D1303634

JE
Burg, Ann E.
Pirate Pickle and the white
 balloon

JAN 1 7 2008

MID-CONTINENT PUBLIC LIBRARY
Riverside Branch
2700 N.W. Vivion Road
Riverside, MO 64150

RS

WITHDRAWN
FROM THE RECORDS OF
MID-CONTINENT PUBLIC LIBRARY

Pirate Pickle
and the
White Balloon

Written by Ann Burg
Illustrated by Marilyn Janovitz

Children's Press
An Imprint of Scholastic Inc.
New York • Toronto • London • Auckland • Sydney
Mexico City • New Delhi • Hong Kong
Danbury, Connecticut

For Celia, who made every day an adventure.
—A. B.

Reading Consultant

Cecilia Minden-Cupp, *PhD*
Former Director of the Language and Literacy Program
Harvard Graduate School of Education
Cambridge, Massachusetts

MID-CONTINENT PUBLIC LIBRARY

3 0000 12941691 7

MID-CONTINENT PUBLIC LIBRARY
Riverside Branch
2700 N.W. Vivion Road
Riverside, MO 64150

RS

Cover design: The Design Lab
Interior design: Herman Adler

Library of Congress Cataloging-in-Publication Data

Burg, Ann E.
  Pirate Pickle and the white balloon / by Ann Burg; illustrated by
Marilyn Janovitz; reading consultant, Cecilia Minden-Cupp.
     p. cm. — (A rookie reader : opposites)
  ISBN-13: 978-0-531-17544-6 (lib. bdg.)   978-0-531-17778-5 (pbk.)
  ISBN-10: 0-531-17544-8 (lib. bdg.)   0-531-17778-5 (pbk.)
  1. English language—Synonyms and antonyms—Juvenile literature.
I. Janovitz, Marilyn, ill. II. Title. III. Series.
  PE1591.B78 2007
  428.1—dc22   2006027033

No part of this publication may be reproduced in whole or in part, or stored in a retrieval
system, or transmitted in any form or by any means, electronic, mechanical, photocopying,
recording, or otherwise, without written permission of the publisher. For information
regarding permission, write to Scholastic Inc., 557 Broadway, New York, NY 10012.

©2007 by Scholastic Inc.
Illustrations ©2007 by Marilyn Janovitz.
All rights reserved. Published simultaneously in Canada.
Printed in China.

SCHOLASTIC, CHILDREN'S PRESS, A ROOKIE READER, and associated logos are
trademarks and/or registered trademarks of Scholastic Inc.
1 2 3 4 5 6 7 8 9 10 R 17 16 15 14 13 12 11 10 09 08

My white balloon is lost.

Wherever can it be?

I've searched all across the land.
Maybe it floated out to sea!

I know a certain pirate.
He wears a black patch on his eye.

**Maybe he grabbed my white balloon
as it floated through the sky.**

9

Maybe my balloon is trapped,
and I must set it free!

I'm not afraid no matter what.
I'm as brave as brave can be!

I will sail all day.

I will sail all night.

Then I will sail over the waves
and under the moon.

I will sail forever
to find my balloon.

When I find Pirate Pickle, I will roar,
"That balloon's mine, not yours!"

Then I will float over the waves
and under the moon.

I will float back home
with my balloon.

My white balloon!

It's stuck in my neighbor's tree!

Excuse me, Mr. Pickle. . . .

Please get it down for me.

Word List (82 words)
(Words in **bold** are used as opposites.)

a	eye	it's	not	the
across	**find**	I've	on	then
afraid	float	know	**out**	through
all	floated	**land**	**over**	to
and	for	**lost**	patch	**trapped**
as	forever	matter	pickle	tree
back	**free**	maybe	pirate	**under**
balloon	get	me	please	waves
balloon's	grabbed	**mine**	roar	wears
be	he	moon	sail	what
black	his	Mr.	**sea**	when
brave	home	must	searched	wherever
can	I	my	set	**white**
certain	I'm	neighbor's	sky	will
day	**in**	**night**	stuck	with
down	is	no	that	**yours**
excuse	it			

About the Author

Ann Burg grew up writing stories for her family and her friends. She wrote articles for newspapers and has always kept a journal. This is her seventh children's book but her drawers are stuffed with many more stories and poems. Ann lives in upstate New York with her husband, two children, one dog, and one very special bear.

About the Illustrator

Marilyn Janovitz's work, in a variety of styles and mediums, has been used in advertising, editorial, and textile design. She is the author-illustrator of many books for children including *Look Out Bird!*, *Is It Time?*, and *What Could Be Keeping Santa?* Marilyn works in her closet-sized studio where she can see the Empire State Building twenty blocks away.